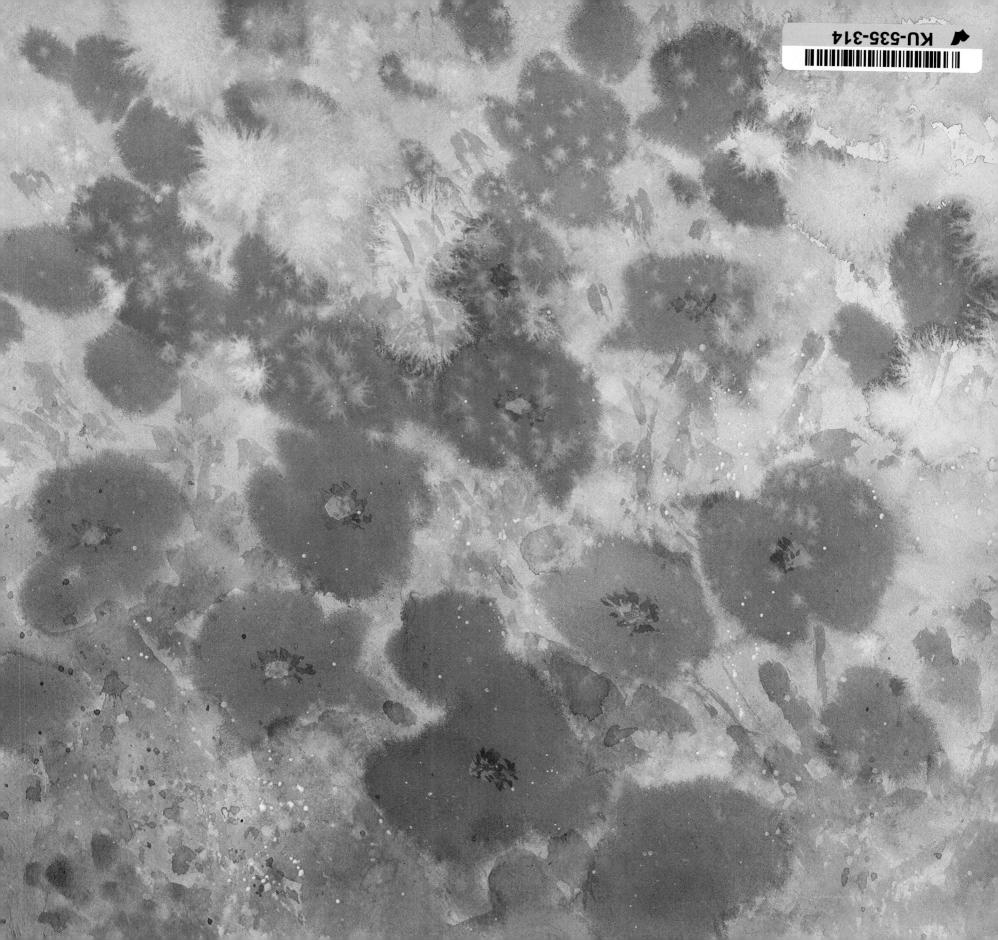

Endpapers:
Poppies. This year, on road-side
verges and in places that have escaped
the herbicide sprays, there has been a
tremendous flush of poppies. I have
painted them without any detail at all
because I was most conscious of
looking at a haze of colours and
shapes. Poppies bring back memories
not just of English watercolour artists
but also of the French Impressionists.
Poppies give so much pleasure that
people will travel some distance to see
them. I am often asked if I have seen
some particularly fine display on a
roadside.

Beningfield's
English
Landscape

Driving back from Halvergate Marshes through Suffolk, very late in the evening, I came to a common with a big, well restored windmill. I have painted it with the last glimmers of light and added the sheep, which were not there, partly recalling the wool trade which was once so important in Suffolk. The painting is an interpretation of what I saw, but I feel that my job is to create moods and atmospheres and sometimes to paint things as I would like them to be.

Beningfield's English Landscape

GORDON BENINGFIELD

VIKING

VIKING

Penguin Books Ltd, Harmondsworth, Middlesex, England
Viking Penguin Inc., 40 West 23rd Street, New York, New York 10010, U.S.A.
Penguin Books Australia Ltd, Ringwood, Victoria, Australia
Penguin Books Canada Ltd, 2801 John Street, Markham, Ontario, Canada L3R 1B4
Penguin Books (N.Z.) Ltd, 182-190 Wairau Road, Auckland 10 New Zealand

First published 1985. Reprinted 1985

Edited by Ian Cameron and Jill Hollis
Designed by Ian Cameron
Produced by Cameron Books, 2a Roman Way, London N7 8XG

Filmset in Linotype Times by Cameron Books
Printed in Holland by Royal Smeets Offset, Weert

British Library Cataloguing in Publication Data available

ISBN 0-670-80202-6

This book is dedicated to my wife Betty and my daughters Sally and Sarah.

This book records my impressions of the English countryside in 1984 and the first half of 1985. My intention was not to make any sort of systematic survey, but to draw and paint places and things that appealed to me, mixing full-scale landscapes with close-ups of plants and animals, and finely detailed pictures with spontaneous, impressionistic studies. For me, the magic of the English landscape lies in its richness, which is conveyed in a million fleetingly expressive moments or specially evocative details. Above all, it is the ordinary things, like this group of cattle near Ashridge on the borders of Hertfordshire and Buckinghamshire, that move me most.

Contents

Pictures

The English Landscape

In the same week in the spring of 1985 that I found myself being set upon by a Dorset farmer with a pitchfork because he did not like me photographing the destruction that was being perpetrated on his land, another small environmental tragedy was being enacted on the other side of the country. A landowner at West Mersea in Essex wanted to build seven houses on a two-acre meadow overlooking the sea. Undisturbed for decades, the site accommodated some 15,000 plants of the green-winged orchid, a species that was never particularly widespread but is now disappearing rapidly because of the ploughing up of the old grasslands that are its habitat. Planning permission for building on the site had expired, and the Nature Conservancy Council opposed the application for its renewal, designating the two acres as a Site of Special Scientific Interest. As a statutory three months had to go by to allow counter-arguments to be put forward before the site could be protected, the NCC also applied to the Department of the Environment for an emergency prevention order. The landowner, however, was quicker than the bureaucrats. One Wednesday evening, after the environmental protesters who had been staging a sit-in beside the meadow had gone home, a three-man team set to work to spray the field with general-purpose herbicide, supervised by the police in the interests of law and order. The landowner was acting within his legal rights, and the site was no longer of special, indeed any, scientific interest.

Stories of this sort now appear with great regularity in the press. Over the past two or three years, scarcely a week has passed without some new tale of confrontation over the environment, like this one from August 1984. Preseli District Council in West Wales was reported in *The Observer* as having destroyed the only colony in Pembrokeshire of the small blue, which happens to be one of the butterfly species most threatened by the onward march of agriculture. In spite of having agreed with the local Naturalists' Trust that the home of the colony, a disused railway cutting by an inlet off Milford Haven, should be preserved, the council buried the colony, which was then at the caterpillar stage, under four feet of clay and rubble from the marina that it was building nearby. The council's director of works commented: 'Apparently we are guilty. We were told it was an area of some sort of naturalist benefit, but we are doing a major civil engineering project and we tipped some mud on top of all those butterflies. Apparently it is only in that little spot that those poor little creatures are living – or were living.' He added that the council was willing to co-operate with the Naturalists' Trust but, 'if they are going to scream every time we turn over a blade of grass, it is going to make life difficult, if not impossible.'

There is just one positive aspect to this story: five years ago, when I was working on *Beningfield's Countryside*, such an occurrence would probably have gone unreported except, perhaps, in the local press. The prominence now given, at least in the serious press, to environmental matters indicates a new level of concern for the countryside and its wildlife. It is no coincidence that in 1985

Marsh marigolds or, as I am more used to calling them, kingcups. One of the most striking sights of spring, they are still quite common in some places but are among the plants that are killed when water meadows are drained.

17

the National Farmers' Union has felt it necessary to beef up its public relations operation and make some tentatively conservationist noises. The new man in charge of public relations was clear about why he was needed: 'The [farming] industry does need a high level of support from the public, who have to be reminded of the positive benefits. I would like them to see farmers as the natural conservators of the countryside.' One wonders whether the aim of the exercise will be to lull us into forgetting the past forty years of destruction.

The 'eighties show every sign of being the decade during which people start to fight back against the destroyers. Unfortunately, public opinion has been awakened too late to save much of the countryside, and we are well into the eleventh hour for the rest. As a painter, I have no desire to chronicle the destruction in my pictures. My aim is to celebrate the beauty of what survives. As a conservationist, I want everyone to understand what has been done, and is being done, to the countryside in the hope that if other people share my anger about it, the devastation can be stopped.

The scale of what has happened is hard to comprehend. It is said that half of our ancient broad-leaved woodlands have been destroyed in the past forty years – more than had disappeared in the previous four centuries – and other losses are even worse: since 1939, 60 per cent of lowland heath has vanished, including 75 per cent of the heathland in Dorset. 80 per cent of chalk downland has gone, along with a scarcely believable 95 per cent of the hay meadows that were once awash with wild flowers.

The destruction started in earnest during World War II, and for a compelling reason: a nation that relied on imports for more than half its food had to become self-sufficient as the war cut off outside sources. The most available method of dramatically increasing food production was bringing much more land into cultivation: moors and heaths and downs were ploughed up. Since the war, governments have been unfailingly eager to sacrifice the countryside to the balance of payments: a panoply of grants, subsidies and tax concessions have encouraged farmers in an orgy of hedge-tearing, pond-draining, chemical-spraying improvements which have turned much of lowland England into an enormous, characterless food factory. Owners of land that was unsuitable for turning into cereal prairies have been offered similar enticements to cover it with Christmas trees, even though the economic benefits to the nation are at best debatable. For the farmers – not so much the struggling hill farmers as the fat cats in the lowlands – our entry into the European Common Market in 1973 provided a new bonanza, with subsidies that keep food prices artificially high at the expense of the taxpayer and add further motivation for farmers to destroy yet more countryside to add to the mountains of over-production. We are in the extraordinary situation that our most subsidised industry, which was supported to the tune of £2 billion in 1983, is the one that is doing most damage to the countryside that is our national heritage. Meanwhile, the equivalent of

So many of the details of early spring are yellow: the pussy willow with its yellow stamens, the lesser celandines and the brimstone, here on honeysuckle leaves, the earliest of our butterflies.

over £36 for every single person in the country is being spent on farming subsidies, more than sixty times as much money as is being spent on conservation.

Forty years ago, in the commentary to a documentary film on the war effort, E.M. Forster wrote of our farmers 'fighting against the forces of nature'. At the time, the image would have seemed touchingly plucky. Since then, though, the armoury available has made the battle shockingly one-sided, with heavy machinery to rip out the hedges and drain anywhere that is unremuneratively damp, and chemicals to kill what cannot be converted into cash. This, and the publicity given to the wild men who will defy anything from preservation orders to High Court injunctions to bulldoze whatever might interrupt their prairies, have left the farmers looking a whole lot less noble.

The debate about conservation and the countryside has shown how little substance there is to most of the arguments against the conservationists. There is, for example, the idea that man has been changing the English landscape for the past 6,000 years, with occasional accelerations in the pace of change, as in the Agricultural Revolution of the late eighteenth and early nineteenth centuries, and that the past forty years have been doing no more than continuing the pattern of progress. What this ignores is the totally different level of technology involved today. The replacement of the open pastures with hedged or walled fields in the Agricultural Revolution may have fundamentally changed the countryside, but it created habitats as well as destroying them. It was not accompanied, like the replacement of the enclosed fields with open prairies, by chemical warfare designed to wipe out every alien plant and frequently eliminating most of the animal population as well. The new countryside is about as welcoming to wildlife as an industrial estate – indeed there are certain similarities, except that an industrial estate provides more employment and releases different pollutants. We should remember that the chemicals that are put on the land are in general either fertilisers or poisons. The nitrates from fertilisers produce ecological havoc in our rivers and often turn up in unhealthy concentrations in our tap water. Poisons, of course, kill the good and the harmless along with the bad and will inevitably finish up, albeit in tiny quantities, in our food. Who is to say what the long-term effects of this contamination might be? It is simply not correct to pass off the new agricultural revolution as the continuation of a tradition of improvement. It is more like the reckless sacrifice of tradition on the altar of short-term gain.

Another argument that surfaces from time to time as a reason for not stopping the farmers doing their worst is that a particular location is not of outstanding beauty – no prettier than lots of other places – and hardly deserves the fuss that is being made about it. But then, to the casual observer, a mudflat can seem like the most featureless place on earth, although it may support multitudes of waterfowl and waders whose arrival can make a place like this seem quite magical. Some of the landowners who wanted to plough up their bits of

The skylark is a bird that I almost inevitably see when I am walking across downland looking at the butterflies. It is one of the characters of the countryside, a brown bird that runs along, hiding itself in the grass, but then lifts off and goes up into the clouds.

Halvergate Marshes in Norfolk described the marshes as flat and boring, as if this justified destroying their unique character in order to add to the cereal mountain. The aesthetic views of the would-be destroyers should carry no weight at all, but it is these opinions that have allowed whole counties in central England to be turned into featureless prairie. Why worry that Huntingdonshire has lost 88 per cent of its hedges or that 90 per cent of Nottinghamshire ponds have been filled in, when there is plenty more of the same elsewhere? Sadly, this is no longer true. The ordinary things of the countryside are well on their way to becoming rarities – it is only too easy to imagine a time when a genuine water-meadow or a hazel coppice with bluebells will seem remarkable enough to be a tourist attraction in much the same way as Gloucester Old Spot Pigs and White Park cattle, saved from extinction by the clear-sighted enthusiasts of the Rare Breeds Survival Trust, draw crowds into farm parks.

The apostles of progress are very keen to point out what a lot of splendid things our new countryside is being used for. A book produced by the Open University and the Countryside Commission presents an aerial photograph of Fernworthy Reservoir in Dartmoor National Park as 'an example of the way in which a limited area is now used for several different purposes. The artificial lake designed for water storage has now been opened up for sailing and fishing. The shoreline . . . has been developed as a picnic site by the South West Water Authority in association with the Forestry Commission who have also provided public access to the conifer plantation, via nature trails and forest walks.' Or to put it differently, two massive intrusions on the landscape of a National Park have been given an overlay of recreational usefulness. The same book offers an even more flagrant commercial along similar lines: 'a Forestry Commission plantation may have a recreational role, may also provide a moderating influence over water catchment, may assist the farmer in acting as a shelter belt for livestock, may create rural employment and may provide a unique environment for many species of flora and fauna, as well as acting as a source of timber.' It may equally obliterate the habitats for the existing wildlife to leave an unsightly monoculture of alien conifers that are remarkable only for how few other animals and plants find a home among them.

Perhaps the most dangerous argument of all, though, uses the idea of balance. The position that the bureaucrats so often fall back on is that of balancing the needs of conservation against the legitimate aspirations of the farmers (which for them as businessmen must be to increase their profits), or of the road hauliers or the builders or the mineral extractors or the tourist industry. But all compromises like this end up as a further erosion of the environment. We have to realise that there is an absolute and urgent need to conserve what is left of the countryside and that every time the authorities do their balancing act and those with legitimate aspirations are given half a cake – which is probably all they have calculated on getting – another piece of our landscape is damaged for ever.

A bleak, open piece of landscape produced by modern farming with the tracks heavily scarred by machinery – though I was quite intrigued here by the texture of grooves made by the wheels. In the distance are the Chilterns. Now that the hills are no longer grazed by sheep, the National Trust is having to clear much of the encroaching hawthorn in an attempt to maintain the habitat for the downland plants and butterflies. The picture was painted in early spring with the lapwings just starting to display.

I drove two hundred miles one day in March looking for the real Cotswolds and finding nothing but a barren vista of modern farming with large, bleak fields and grass bearing the yellowish scars caused by recent applications of Paraquat. However, I did find this scene on the River Windrush with pollarded willows and the church, as so often, dominating the centre of the village.

It was equally difficult to find a village that was not ridiculously dolled up. The furthest from the usual expense-account picturesque scene was this corner of Hampnett, which did not have an immaculately kept village green but a proper common that was a piece of rough, hilly grazing land with a stream running through it and a scatter of houses around the edge. In the background, the rooks were beginning to build their nests in the bare trees.

A ruined smithy on the outskirts of an almost uninhabited village in Cambridge-shire. Inside, you could still see the furnace, what was left of the bellows, and bits of iron lying around. It was at the stage when the vegetation was just taking over and beginning to swallow it up, but you could still see remnants of the past and of the activity that went on there. Even though nature is, in a sense, healing the wound left by human occupancy, you are still very conscious of the place's history.

English elm trees growing out of the hedgerows used to be one of the common sights of the English landscape until they were wiped out in the 'seventies by Dutch elm disease. It was to see and sketch one of the few survivors that I went to Cambridgeshire.

I was sitting in a West Country meadow looking at some common blues on a grassy bank with a hedgerow behind me, and I was not aware of any livestock in the field on the other side. Then I heard a snorting and grunting and looked round to see a pig with its head stuck through the hedge, obviously wondering what I was up to. An irresistible subject.

On the opposite page is a study of my friend Alan the shepherd in the lambing yard he builds for himself each year. He is the only shepherd I know who works in a completely traditional way, rearing Hampshire Down sheep only a few miles from my home. Here he is in spring with twin lambs and the proud Hampshire Down ewe looking on.

Robins. In all the landscapes that I have painted, whatever the county or the time of year, there have been few in which I have not been accompanied by a robin. I could almost guarantee that within a few minutes of my settling down to sketch there would be a robin around somewhere.

Memories

The River Ver in Hertfordshire, near St Albans.

Although the six pictures in this chapter show places in Hertfordshire as they are today, they are linked together because of the special memories they hold for me. In the forty-five years I have lived here, a quiet countryside of small mixed farms has been gnawed away by housing, industry and roads, and much of what is left has suffered from the activities of the farmers.

For this book, as always, I have been searching for the bits of landscape that have managed to survive largely unharmed. One of my starting points has been my childhood memories. Wondering whether any of my childhood haunts were still recognisable, I went on a pilgrimage to a couple of spots on the River Ver that I remember particularly liking.

Back in the late 'forties, when I was ten or eleven, there was a stretch of the Ver near St Albans where my friends and I spent many a long day during our summer holidays. You can tell just how good a place it was from the fact that we were willing to walk three miles, which seemed to us like a very long way, to reach it. We would always take sandwiches, either jam or fish-paste, and a bottle of water with us. Once in a while, one of us would have a bottle of Tizer, but that was a special treat.

We would spend all day there playing in the water, fishing and generally having a good time. The one disadvantage of the place was the leeches — every quarter of an hour or so, we had to leap out and pick them off our legs. The river had a stony bottom, and we used to wear black plimsolls, without socks, so that we could rush around in it without hurting our feet. By the time we got home again, our shoes would be quite dry — in my memory, every day in those childhood summers seems to have been warm and sunny.

Going back to the same spot after so many years, I was pleased to find that the river and the water meadow leading down to it were very much as I remembered them, although the trees were perceptibly older and there were definitely fewer of them. The river itself was still reasonably clear and stony. There was perhaps more hawthorn along the banks, but the place has retained much of its charm — I was lucky that I returned there on a sunny day. The big change, though, was in getting there. This time, I arrived along traffic-laden roads. Back in the 'forties, there was very little need to walk carefully at the side of the road to avoid getting run over, because we would literally have seen only one or two cars.

There is another place on the River Ver that I remember from my childhood, further upstream, near Redbourne. This was a simple bridge on a lane that led to a farm. Watching some children playing there, I remembered myself almost forty years ago. In those days, you could buy a cane, a piece of green twine, a very primitive float and a hook, all for a shilling. With this equipment, we spent long hours catching small fish like minnows and gudgeon as well as enjoying ourselves just messing around in the water. I love this sort of place —

an unassuming little corner that is so typical of the English countryside, and yet can easily be lost because it is not sufficiently important for anyone to worry about protecting it.

The bridge and its surroundings still look, at first sight, very much as they did, but it would be wrong to say that everything is exactly as it was. Apart from the nitrates that are applied to the land as fertilisers and have filtered into almost all our rivers, the Ver has suffered very badly from the fact that it loses enormous amounts of water near its source to provide for the needs of Luton. This is supposed to be a short-term measure, but meanwhile, the river is sometimes reduced to a trickle, and I suspect that a lot of damage will have been done before the pumping stops and the river is restored to its full volume. For the moment, though, some of the water meadows and places like those I have painted survive and still provide a home for small mammals and, in winter, for snipe.

The second pair of pictures in this chapter represent rather more recent memories: a sketch and a painting showing two views of St Albans, which I always think of as my home town. When I was working as an ecclesiastical artist, I used to walk through the district called Romeland once or twice a day, and I always liked the contrast between the simple cottages there and the grandeur of the abbey behind. It is a very quiet part of town and does not seem to have changed much.

The final two sketches are of Little Gaddesden church, a few miles away from my cottage, on the edge of Ashridge. Like any old church, it again recalls memories of my life as an ecclesiastical artist. As I went around working in country churches, I often took the opportunity of sketching the outside and the landscape around for my own pleasure as well as doing whatever I had come to do inside, working for instance on the stained glass or the pews or the vestments. But this church also brings back a more recent event: my daughter was married there this spring. I was pleased that she chose a church tucked away out in the countryside and could have a real country wedding. Churches for me are another essential part of the English landscape, just as much so as the hedgerows or the wildlife. Here we are looking across meadows to the church past the old beech trees that are typical of the area. Some of them have gone, because beech trees, with their shallow roots, are very vulnerable to the occasional dry summer, and others are beyond their peak, which is, of course, no reason to remove them. Elderly trees, and dead ones, are usually best left where they are unless there is some very pressing reason for doing otherwise. After all, a dead tree has almost as important a part to play as a live one, harbouring all manner of lichens and insects and birds, then eventually crumbling away and becoming part of the soil.

The River Ver near Redbourne, Hertfordshire.

St Alban's Abbey and cottages at Romeland.

Two sketches of Little Gaddesden church.

41

My Garden

I was prompted to paint this series of pictures of the flowers in my garden by listening to *Gardeners' Question Time* on the radio last May. They were talking, as so often, about all the marvellous chemicals you can use to get rid of the wild flowers that gardeners are not supposed to want. In particular, they were talking about how to blast all the daisies and speedwell and dandelions out of your lawn. I glanced out of the window to see the whole of my lawn covered in these flowers and thought how much better it looked than it would if they had been killed off. I felt that the best thing I could do would be to paint a couple of pictures of the lawn, and I went on from there to record other plants that I particularly like in the garden.

I can appreciate formal gardens for the skill that goes into their management – they can look wonderful around an Elizabethan manor house. But for my cottage garden, I prefer to think about the people who might have lived here in the past. They would certainly not have had the time to do much gardening, except perhaps to grow their own food, because they had to earn a living. If you look at early watercolours, you will see cottages almost swallowed up by wild vegetation with the odd foxglove or hollyhock poking up out of the wilderness. I try to encourage something of this atmosphere here, and as a result the garden attracts birds and butterflies.

My idea of gardening is just about as far as you can get from the world of *Gardeners' Question Time*. I plant very little – many of my favourites plants, such as honesty and Chinese lanterns, come up by themselves year after year. I regularly plant marigolds, because I love their brilliant colour, and when people bring me cowslips and primroses which would otherwise be destroyed, I will put them in here, there and everywhere. I try to keep some buddleia going for the butterflies, but it really prefers poor, dry soil – it is even happy growing out of old walls – and does not do well in the rather damp valley soil. It suffers badly in winter from the heavy frosts that we have here.

We cut the small areas of lawn at the front and back of the house, but do very little beyond minor management when the trees are beginning to overshadow each other and there is a danger of losing some of them. I have no desire to grow fine flowers to decorate the house; I prefer the common wild flowers like the cow parsley that grows on the Moor outside. Another favourite is the great hairy willowherb, which grows there by the river and is a mass of pink flowers in late July and early August.

At this moment, in July, the garden is getting a little too overgrown, and I need to cut it back a bit so that there will be some variety, with patches of sunlight to contrast with the lush, shady growth. Quite apart from the natural history aspects of the garden, I just try to create an impression of the way it might have been a century or so ago, when there was no machinery to keep it all pristine and organised. The charm of an old cottage should be not just in the building itself, but in its surroundings as well.

Lawn with dandelions, daisies and speedwell.

An orange spread: orange tip on flowering honesty, marigolds, and Chinese lanterns with honesty seedcases.

In the old orchard behind the massive hazel hedge, I do nothing at all beyond taking a scythe to it here and there later in the year. The heavy frosts literally knock down the vegetation. Nature copes very well with these things – the wild world can manage itself better than I could ever do it. I am content to look on and hope to learn something.

Apple blossom is as much part of England for me as the rooks in March, the cuckoo in spring or the sound of church bells. I have treated this lovely apple blossom from my orchard as a very free sketch to catch some of the softness of spring. Many of my apples are very old varieties, so old that I do not know what many of them are, but these elderly trees are loaded with fruit each year. I like their gnarled shapes, full of holes and crevices where birds nest and brimstones hibernate. The most plentiful butterflies in the garden and the orchard are the small tortoiseshells, peacocks and red admirals that breed on the nettles in front of the cottage, as do commas, which also breed on the wild hops that grow in some of the hedges. In addition, we get wall butterflies as well as holly blues because of the ivy and the holly trees, and a few meadow browns, as we are on the fringe of meadow land. Last year, a white admiral passed through and landed briefly in the back garden; a few live in small patches of woodland not far from here.

Among the nicest sights, though, are the orange tips which breed on the garlic mustard plants that I encourage here in the early spring. This year, the butterflies have flown on well into July because of the rather late season that everything has had. I like to see them on the honesty plants, taking nectar from the mauve flowers. Later in the year, the honesty produces its decorative seed-cases, which I have painted with Chinese lanterns because they go together so well when they are dried – I remember seeing vases of them in cottage windows when I was a boy, and we still use them in this way.

Our bird population includes spotted flycatchers, nuthatches, greater spotted woodpeckers, and tree creepers, which are often to be found on my pear tree. In winter, we are visited by goldcrests and long-tailed tits. This year, we have had more blackcaps than usual; they have sung right through the spring and into the summer. We have also had the beautiful sight of a turtle dove which I saw gritting on the track in front of the house and later heard calling. Among larger birds, we have tawny owls, mainly in winter; barn owls are seen only very occasionally, further up the valley. Also in winter, we have snipe and woodcock coming through. The woodcocks flutter in over the cottage and drop down in the reeds. Across the river, the population of the rookery is now increasing. Although farm managers do not want to have the rooks around, the owners of the estate now think differently, and rook shooting has stopped here, but the birds still have to contend, like everything else in the country-side, with the ever-mounting effects of farm chemicals. I believe that any damage caused by rooks is outweighed by the good they do in gobbling up insects.

One of the plants that gardeners are fanatical about pulling up is bindweed, in spite of its glorious flowers. The point about bindweed is that you need to have lots of it to make a show. When you have a mass of white trumpets, it looks wonderful. For my painting, it has given me a colour scheme to which I have often returned: a white flower and a white butterfly, in this case the large bindweed and large white.

The insects on the rough vegetation of the Moor in front of my cottage are an inexhaustible subject for me, and I have made drawing after drawing of them, as this is the way to study anything from life and capture the essence of its character. This series of a sketch, a working drawing and a painting shows small tortoiseshells and bumble bees on cow parsley in late spring.

51

Small tortoiseshells and bumble bees
on cow parsley.

Home Ground

This picture was the result of a walk up the River Gade from my home on a very frosty, bitterly cold day. The white sun trying to break through the chilly mist illuminated an almost monochrome landscape.

Looking across from the Gade to my cottage on the Moor in winter. When I am coming back from walking my Scottish deerhound Bruce across the fields in the late afternoon, the light in the window makes me want to get back and toast crumpets by the fire.

Bulrushes on the banks of the Gade. The thick vegetation provides perfect cover for the birds, which include water rail as well as the more common coots, moorhens, mallards and dabchicks. The gates date back to the days before the whole river was fished: they were locked at certain times to keep would-be fishermen out. Because the Gade is fed by a spring, it is not polluted, and visitors are amazed by the size of the trout that can be caught in it.

A short distance up the Gade from my cottage is Great Gaddesden, a village with close personal associations for me – my father is buried in the church-yard and my daughter lives up the hill behind the church. The farmyard to the left of the picture is where the cruck barn that I drew for *Beningfield's Country-side* used to be. Now it is just a heap of rubble thanks to the lethargy of the planning authorities which allow listed buildings to be demolished. Now we are in danger of losing the adjoining barn on the same site. Sometimes I think that the planners are doing such a bad job that it would be better if they handed things over to writers and artists.

This is a track on the Halsey estate, near my home. It is somewhere I often walk, and it is where I can usually find plenty of holly with berries for Christmas. A couple of years ago, though, when I went to gather holly, it had been completely stripped – in the few days since my previous visit, the fieldfares had been there, though of course I did not grudge them the berries.

A part-wooden cottage for a worker on the Halsey estate. It has appealed to me as long as I have lived in the area, partly because its simplicity fits in so well with the background of woodland.

Buckinghamshire cottages, with one or two old oak trees covered in ivy and the other a real tea-cosy affair with no upstairs windows. This must be of some age, as many of the early cottages were built like this, although some, including my own, would have had an upper storey with windows added subsequently. While I was standing there sketching, I could hear the voice of an old lady coming from inside. I expect she was wondering what sort of an idiot could be staring at her house.

Horse chestnuts in May. Although they are often planted and appear in rather managed countryside, I like them not just for their blossom but also for their naturally tidy shape .

Looking out from the Chilterns towards Buckinghamshire, across arable land dotted with beech trees to downland in the distance.

Lanes and Hedgerows

A painting of a Buckinghamshire lane and the sketches for it. The tree is an old oak, which looks rather as if it has been pollarded at some time, but its thick covering of ivy has made it club-shaped. Trees like this are great for nesting birds and hibernating butterflies. The landscape with the lane going off across the rolling countryside and the farm tucked away in the bottom of the valley is typical of the area.

Many of the lanes in this part of south-west Hertfordshire are rather ancient, with deep banks. This is a lane that I often cycle down towards the church at Great Gaddesden. Although the hedges here have been trimmed mechanically, they are still of interest except for the few gaps where they have been destroyed by straw burning.

January just up the lane from my cottage. The big hedgerow oak, leafless against a winter sky, contrasts with the dark green foliage of the holly.

Wild arum, better known as 'lords-and-ladies' or 'cuckoo pint'. It is easy to see in such a strikingly sculptural form why Henry Moore, with his great love of the countryside, has always been influenced by shapes from nature.

A typical Buckinghamshire lane at the end of May, shaded by an oak tree and bordered with cow parsley. As you cycle or walk along, the fresh life of this time of year seems to cascade out of the banks at you. In many ways, this very simple scene has for me all the feeling of England.

74

Local Hertfordshire sketches: a construction in a hedgerow that people but not cattle can get through and, behind it, a farmworker's cottage with washing hanging out on the line; winter fields with rooks; a delightful stile leading enticingly through a thick hedgerow.

Sussex

In the foreground are some fine post and rail fencing and rough meadow with ox-eye daisies, but the real reason for painting a picture of this part of East Sussex is the elm trees that are so eye-catching on the skyline. In Hertford-shire and most of the Home Counties, virtually all the elm trees have been lost, but East Sussex has done an admirable job of preserving them.

This windmill is near Tangmere in Sussex. It is not used now but has been nicely restored and dominates the landscape from its position up on a hill. I believe that it was used as an ARP look-out post during the war.

At the bottom of the South Downs not far from Chichester is this tiny, simple church, known as the Shepherds' Church. Apart from the romantic associations of the building itself, I have tried in this picture to capture the atmosphere of the warm summer day when I was there – the mist was beginning to clear and I could just see the outline of the downs in the distance.

80

The churchyard of the Shepherds' Church, dotted with old tombstones. As I sat working on this picture, I could imagine hearing the heavy boots of the shepherds as they walked through the little porch.

Near Steyning: a sweep of the Sussex Downs, which are for me the most dramatic of all our downlands.

Looking across from the top of the South Downs, again near Steyning, towards agricultural land in the valley, with more of the expanse of downs rising out of the slight mist in the distance. There are still some sheep grazing on the down-land here, as there would have been for centuries, but today this sight is very much the exception. Very little of the South Downs remains that has escaped destruction by the plough.

Wiltshire

The broad, open landscape of Wiltshire, with the village of Mere. I think of Wiltshire as an ancient landscape because there is so much evidence of Iron Age fortresses and earthworks. On this particular day, I was attracted by the sky – always an important element in such a landscape – which was changing rapidly as I watched. At the moment of the picture, there is sunshine around Mere but evidence of rain falling a few miles beyond the landscape you can see. When I am working on a landscape, I do studies of skies, working with the brush and paper very wet so that I can see which one I might wish to use in the final picture. The studies of Wiltshire skies show the changes that took place over a few minutes.

A Wiltshire landscape in autumn, with a wide open sky, distant suggestions of hill forts, tight clumps of beech trees and, on the right, the strip lynchets of the old agricultural system. The trees were probably planted for shooting, and it is certainly for this reason that they have been allowed to survive when so much of Wiltshire has been ploughed up and ruined. This picture represents the rolling Wiltshire landscape as it has been – indeed, as it ought to be.

On the opposite page, a chapel in a Wiltshire village.

90

In the same Wiltshire village as the chapel was a group of thatched cottages with an old apple tree, which is the subject of the sketch. The atmosphere was very much that of the last century, and the scene is one that would have appealed to many a nineteenth-century artist.

Dorset

Staying with a friend in Dorset, I looked out of my bedroom window very early one morning, hoping to catch sight of roe deer, and I was entranced by the Turnerish sight of the misty air and the sun just coming up. I have loved the paintings of Turner ever since I was a schoolboy, and without in any sense copying him, which I would not want to do, I wanted to capture some of the same feeling.

The study of the sky is from the same morning as the landscape but with the sun rather higher.

I have known Powerstock Forest for sixteen years or more. I first went there because of two people: Thomas Hardy, because it was an important part of the landscape that inspired his work, and Kenneth Allsop, who was just having his great battle with the Forestry Commission. They were starting to clear-fell it so that they could plant the inevitable cash crop of Christmas trees, but Allsop managed to stop them in their tracks. Perhaps by managing to intimidate them through being more coherent and more knowledgeable about the natural history value of this woodland than any member of the Forestry Commission, he saved ninety to a hundred acres of this ancient forest.

Lying at the base of Eggardon Hill in south-west Dorset, Powerstock Forest is something that the Forestry Commission classed as a useless, scrubby area. The aged sessile oaks with their spreading, mossy branches were obviously not a commercial proposition, but the combination of oak trees with hazel coppice is characteristically English, though it is rare to find any today that is as unspoilt as this. The age of the forest is reflected in the richness of its wild-life. The dormouse is still to be found, and fallow deer can be glimpsed among the trees. Birds of prey sweep across the canopy: buzzards, hobbies, kestrels and, particularly, sparrowhawks. The forest flowers include orchids, and in spring there is a carpet of bluebells. Among the shafts of sunlight fly uncommon butterflies: marsh fritillaries, wood whites and silver-washed fritillaries – all totally useless to the Forestry Commission.

The next stage in the saga was that the Forestry Commission, stuck with something that had been designated as a Site of Special Scientific Interest, decided to off-load it on the commercial market, which would have left the dirty work of destroying the forest to others. Fortunately, at this point, Miss Brotherton of the Dorset County Naturalists' Trust stepped in and formed the Silver Jubilee Committee, a group of writers, landowners, naturalists, painters and sculptors with an interest in the area – people like Sir Peter Scott, John Fowles, Dame Elisabeth Frink, Jack Hargreaves and myself – first to acquire the forest and then to buy up and preserve more land of similar quality. At long last, then, Powerstock Forest is completely safe. The total area that we have bought is some 250 acres. I was there in May and had the satisfaction of watching a Manpower Services team with chainsaws clear-felling the horrible conifers and burning them on site. I only wish that Kenneth Allsop had been alive to see it. The hope is that, with some coaxing, the forest of sessile oaks will regenerate to cover the whole area, a process that will take many, many years because a wild forest cannot be created overnight. But at least the wild-life is there on the original hundred acres and will spread out across the rest. A few small patches of conifers will remain, partly because the money they can produce will help the rest of the scheme and partly because in small quantities they can add to the diversity of the landscape. In the painting, which I have donated to the Silver Jubilee Trust, I have tried to show something of the

essence of the forest, the mysterious, rather eerie sessile oaks, the bluebells and the fallow deer.

The saving of Powerstock Forest is a lovely success story, but it's important to put it into perspective. The hundred acres of unspoilt forest is only a fragment, the size of an East Anglian farmer's prairie field. I had an unforgettable reminder of the wider realities when I left the now protected forest and drove two miles up the road with a friend. There, we were confronted by the sight of land being totally destroyed with bulldozers and lorries: hedges were being ripped out and burned, trees pulled down and little water meadows being drained. I got out of the car and stood in the lane to take a photograph. Before I could take another, I was set upon by the farmer with a pitchfork, which he stuck between my legs and used to pull me away from the hedge – a ridiculous situation, followed by much abuse. But the message in the devastation was quite clear: places like Powerstock Forest could easily end up as oases in a desert of agribusiness. In one sense, this will make their value even greater, as they will be all that we have left of value in the countryside. But in a more important sense, their value will be reduced as they are sealed off by what is around them, and they become defensive enclaves vulnerable to attack, whether by pollution of the water table by fertilisers or by the poisons that can waft over from the activities of the crop sprayers. Like any other reserve or Site of Special Scientific Interest, the forest can only be as good as the countryside around it.

A perfect example of my favourite sort of Dorset landscape, very enclosed, with thick hedgerows, lots of vegetation and a track leading first to a gate and then off into the distance.

This Dorset scene is the sort of West Country landscape that is utterly typical, but is now only to be found in certain areas. It has all the elements: the cottage, grazing cattle, hedgerows, groups of trees and a gentle hillside in the background. The sky has the sort of movement and colour that you get when there is a stormy atmosphere with patches of sunlight.

A Dorset countryside cameo with a drinking trough and a gate off its hinges leaning beside a track. Sometimes it is a ramshackle quality about an old gate or fence that makes it seem especially endearing.

Looking down from a gateway by a hedgerow to a sunlit Dorset coombe. As you can see only part of it, you are tempted down to explore.

Dorset heathland is one of the most fragile habitats that we have left. I had walked down a long path between gorse bushes. When I had got as far as I could go, I looked round to see how far I would have to walk back and found just the subject I was looking for. Quite apart from being the home of such rarities as the Dartford warbler, the smooth snake and the sand lizard, this heathland has a unique atmosphere that makes it well worth preserving.

Heathland again, this time near the coast. The atmosphere is still murky with haze and sea mist, but it is just beginning to clear.

Unlike much of Dorset, the landscape in this part of the Frome Valley, very close to Dorchester, is flat. The farm is one that I have passed many times over the years and always seems to have a flock of sheep in front of it.

Halvergate
Marshes

Halvergate Marshes lie between the Rivers Bure and Yare, on the Norfolk Broads, just inland from Great Yarmouth. The place is different from the landscapes that I usually like to paint – the close-knit hedgerows and meadows or the rolling downlands – but one that I found instantly exciting: the huge skies with their horizons punctuated by windmills, some restored, some derelict, and the flat expanses of marshland grazed in the traditional way by sheep and cattle. But Halvergate Marshes are more than just a romantic landscape, they are the largest uninterrupted stretch of unspoilt marshland left in England.

Used for centuries as rough grazing land, the marshes have developed their own particular character, and one that is to a large extent shaped by man. During their history, the dykes have been dug and the pump mills constructed; the grazing will have determined the balance of the plant life. But despite all this, and the fact that the network of dykes and the gaunt silhouettes of the pump mills are there as constant reminders, you can almost forget how large a part human intervention has played in the creation of this landscape, because it has happened on a scale that has left plenty of room for nature rather than aiming to drive it out. The impression you get on the marshes is one of harmony.

Yet it is exactly this harmony that is under threat – the same threat of drainage and ploughing up for arable use that has claimed half of our wetlands since 1939. During the time that I have been working on this book, other wetlands have been endangered by plans for drainage, among them Derwent Ings, the stretch of watermeadows that runs for twelve miles along the lower Derwent valley in Yorkshire, a 2,500 acre chunk of the Somerset Levels and countless other smaller and less publicised areas, which are in their way no less important, often representing the last enclaves to have escaped being laid waste by the improvers. In the main, the destruction of the British countryside has not been conducted on a grand scale but in innumerable localised mopping-up operations that can seem insignificant but cumulatively add up to disaster for the environment.

The case of Halvergate, though, was one of the few environmental issues that received widespread press coverage, partly because of its size – 10,000 acres at risk – and partly because it so clearly exposed the inadequacies of the 1981 Wildlife and Countryside Act. It also showed how nothing in the countryside is ever definitively saved. In 1982, the Government was claiming that it had saved the area by its refusal to put up the money for the purchase of new pumps to drain the land for ploughing. By 1984, though, some of the landowners in the area had worked out that it would pay them to plough up the marshland anyway. The solution for 1985 was a joint Countryside Commission and Ministry of Agriculture initiative to pay the landowners £50 per acre per year, literally as protection money, for not ploughing up their land, and to take legal action against those who do. This neat demonstration that there is money to be made by farmers who threaten to drive a tractor through the 1981 Act means that parts of Halvergate Marshes have been saved for the moment and at a price.

Sketches of mills on the edge of Halvergate Marshes, which I developed into the paintings that appear on the next spread.

A pump mill on the edge of Halvergate Marshes, where there is arable land,
on which some gulls are feeding.

Another pump mill on the edge of the marshes, this one on the River Bure.

A typical Norfolk church dominating the skyline on the edge of Halvergate Marshes, with a rather threatening, stormy sky looming up behind. Big churches like this date back to the fifteenth and sixteenth centuries, when East Anglia was rich from the wool trade.

112

Halvergate Marsh
roy 84

I wanted to catch the feeling of a perfect late summer day on the marshes. Instead of the strong gusts that you would expect in such a windswept spot, there was no more than a warm, gentle breeze coming in off the sea. I tried to emphasise this in the painting by showing the slight movement of the trees in an otherwise very plain landscape.

114

Halvergate Marshes.

Sheep grazing on the marshes. The fencing has been taken right down into the dyke so that the sheep cannot slip round the end of it.

Broken fencing. It was late in the day, and the weather on the marshes was beginning to change.

A sketch for my painting of the last glint of light over the marshes. With the sheep grazing in the foreground and the derelict pump mill in the distance, this was another landscape with strong overtones of the nineteenth century.

The Last glint.
Halvergate Marsh
1984.

The last glint, Halvergate Marshes.

Farming

❦

On a small farm only a couple of miles from where I live, there are two gigantic Gloucester Old Spot pigs. Although the Gloucester Old Spot is a rare breed, I am sure that it will have a future when pigs are released from their concrete cells and allowed to live decently in the open air. Something rather hardier and more versatile than the Landrace and the Large White will be needed, and the Gloucester Old Spot with its hairy coat could be just the thing. In the past, it was very much a cottager's pig, which used to forage in orchards and on bits of rough ground. My sketch has transported an enormous Old Spot to its proper surroundings of an orchard, where it is chomping up vast quantities of fallen apples.

The Yorkshire landscape at Holme-on-Spalding Moor, which lies more or less half way between Hull and York, is absolutely flat, with just the sort of rich lowland soil that is most tempting to investors in agribusiness. Anyone with an eye to financial profit could see that Holme-on-Spalding Moor would be the perfect place for a cereal prairie.

But here, unlikely though it may seem, there is a farm that still uses horse power. It is not run by some bunch of trendies wanting to live the good life or to get back to nature, but is owned by a family that has always worked with horses. The two generations that now have the farm are working it in the traditional ways they grew up with and still prefer to more mechanised methods. With only a couple of employees to help them, the farmer and his two sons work a modest area of arable land. It is probably no more than two hundred acres – not enough to be considered an economic unit by the exponents of high-tech agriculture, but certainly enough to afford the family a life-style with present-day luxuries, a far cry from the subsistence-level existence that an outsider might expect to find on a wholeheartedly unmodernised farm.

Rejecting the hideous machinery that would be needed to turn their land into a prairie, they still have their hedgerows and little spinneys, and intend to keep them. Their hedges are properly laid – a country skill I have always admired – and there are the beginnings of a laid hedge around the farmhouse. The house's front lawn is covered with molehills, indeed the whole farm abounds with moles which feed off the millions of earthworms you find in soil that is as rich as this in organic matter. You can see the superb condition of the soil from its wonderful dark colour when it is being ploughed.

At harvest time, the binder is pulled by a pair of horses. Behind them large numbers of swallows dive down to catch the insects that have been disturbed by the harvesting. The ducks preening among the stubble were a picturesque detail that demanded to be put in a picture – in the winter, I saw the same ducks being herded around by the farm's sheepdog, just like rather recalcitrant sheep.

The sight of a pair of horses being used in harvesting – something I have never seen before – was unforgettable, the more so because it was not being done for show but as part of the normal routine of people who really know what they are doing and would not dream of working any other way. You can see this in the attention they pay to the well-being of their animals: when they are working, they plan it so that they can stop repeatedly to rest the horses. One December day, I watched them ploughing: they started early and took only a short break in the middle of the day, so that they could have the horses tucked up in the stables before it got too cold and dark. The animals themselves were real working horses rather than perfect specimens of their breeds: in the team of six that were used for ploughing, there were Shires, Clydesdales and at least one with some Percheron in it.

In the farmyard at Holme-on-Spalding Moor. A cart with a broken wheel has been taken over by the chickens, two of which are shown in more detail at the bottom of the picture.

Harvest time at Holme-on-Spalding Moor, with ducks preening among the stubble.

A few minutes of rest during the harvesting.

Making a rick at Holme-on-Spalding Moor, with a trailer drawn by one of the heavy horses. I can just about remember seeing the same sort of scene, with people building ricks from the backs of hay wagons, in Hertfordshire towards the end of the war.

Early in the morning at Holme-on-Spalding Moor: the horses are being tacked up by the farmer before going out to plough. The horse at the right, which has French blood in it, has rather short, stumpy legs. All of them are quiet gentle animals with plenty of power when it is needed. It was a unique chance for me to draw all the working harness actually being used. You can go to a show and see it, but there must be few other places where you can see the equipment and animals in action rather than just appearing in a display or competition.

Ploughing at Holme-on-Spalding Moor. This team of six heavy horses was being controlled by a single farmworker, one of the farmer's sons. You could hear him calling each of them by name, directing them individually.

131

Preserving
the Countryside

The nettle-leaved bellflower or 'bats-in-the-belfry'. This plant is also known as throatwort from its use as a herbal remedy for sore throats and tonsilitis. It is a flower that grows in hedgrows and on the edges of woods. This one, which I found in Sussex, attracted me because of its vibrant blue colour.

A small white butterfly. I have drawn the vegetation in blue crayon with a blue wash to play it down and so highlight the cream and white colour of the butterfly.

Meadow browns on scabious in a hay meadow in Hertfordshire. Traditional hay meadows have become quite rare, but they are delightful places. In midsummer, they are filled with all sorts of wild flowers, and around these you can sometimes find literally thousands of meadow browns.

While the farm at Holme-on-Spalding Moor was an unforgettable experience for me, the purpose of this book is not, of course, to say that all farms should be like it or to preach a return to horse power. The impression that I carried away with me was one of people loving their work and caring for their land. It is their respect for the environment that we should expect all farmers to share. What is bad is not machinery in itself but what is done with it: access to bull-dozers and ditch-digging machines should not inspire a farmer to start acting like Attila the Hun towards his land and its wildlife.

Ultimately, virtually all the threats to the environment can be traced back to self-interest, whether on the part of individuals, companies, local authorities or governments. Often, this is financial, as it is for farmers or developers who want to improve their profits; sometimes it may have to do with prestige or with recreation.

It is not realistic to expect people or bodies altruistically to abandon their self-interest for the general good. However persuasive the case is against, for instance, a pesticide, there is always going to be someone who will say that it is his land and he can pour what he likes on it. When circumstances are as desperate as they are for our landscape and wildlife, the fashion for voluntary controls is a waste of time, a breathing space in which the vandals can go on acting the same way as before. The standard way of dealing with threats to the environment or to public health is consult all the interested parties, the villains as well as the idealists, and then to come up with a voluntary code of practice. But now, where the environment is concerned, it is too late to wait and see whether everyone will be good.

There are plenty of examples of the course of events. Consultations with the motor industry and the petrol manufacturers have allowed a prolonged rearguard action to be fought against tighter controls on lead emission, and quantities of lead continue to be poured into the atmosphere in spite of its toxic effects, especially on children. It is a proven fact that the mute swan population has been decimated through poisoning by lead weights from fishing lines. Consultations with angling bodies have resulted in the fishermen being urged, voluntarily of course, to use alternatives, which it turns out that they do not much fancy. Meanwhile swans continue to be poisoned. At the moment, a combination of paint manufacturers and yachtsmen's organisations from the Royal Yachting Association downwards are campaigning against moves to ban antifouling paints based on tributyl tin, a substance said to be harmful to the Pacific oyster which is raised commercially in several estuaries where yachts are moored. Ignoring the fact that a toxic substance released in the water to kill barnacles and limpets is probably going to have bad effects on other marine life, the yachting fraternity is up in arms against this potential infringement of its liberty. The devastation wrought by straw burning in the hot, dry summers of the early 'eighties led to voluntary guidelines being produced by the National

Wayside flowers: white campion and, on the opposite page, ox-eye daisies and hawkweed.

Autumn. The rich red of hawthorn
berries, and dry leaves that have
blown down and become entangled in
the branches of the hawthorn.

Farmers' Union to fend off statutory controls, but each summer still leaves hedgerows up and down the country burnt to a crisp. DDT is an insecticide celebrated for its tendency to get into food chains and was withdrawn from the market by a voluntary agreement between the Ministry of Agriculture and the British Agrochemicals Association, which represents pesticide manufacturers. Nevertheless, in the spring of 1985, a member of Friends of the Earth was able to buy five-gallon drums of it over the counter in Worcestershire. Although DDT is banned in most developed countries, it continues to be manufactured in Britain for export to the Third World, and it is not illegal for it to be sold here. A Ministry of Agriculture official, reported *The Guardian*, admitted that its 'gentlemen's agreement' had apparently been broken.

It would be nice to think that some lead in the direction of enlightenment was being given by the government, but the reverse is true. Faced with the news that three of England's major water authorities are dispensing tap water that contains nitrate levels in excess of those laid down in recent EEC rules, the reaction has been to exempt them from the controls. At present, the government is showing a marked lack of alarm about acid rain, claiming as a reason for its inactivity that further study is needed. Undoubtedly it is, but this is no excuse to sit back while the effects of pollution produced in England are visited on the lakes and forests of Scandinavia and Germany. Some of it, however, seems to be coming home to roost: a Swedish expert travelling from London to Bristol in August 1985 did not find a single healthy beech tree, and the symptoms, which he knew well from his own experience, indicated that the damage has been taking place over the last twelve to fifteen years. In July 1985, the Transport Secretary announced that the government was over-riding the decision of a joint committee of members of parliament and peers by setting in motion legislation allowing the bypass to Okehampton in Devon to cut into the Dartmoor National Park, along a route supported by the farmers, the road hauliers and tourist interests. Even the statutory protection afforded to national parks, the strongest given to any part of the landscape, can be set aside if the pressure groups ranged against it are influential and vocal enough.

Where positive steps have been taken by the government or its satellites, they can usually be traced back to the efforts of environmental groups and campaigning journalists. The steps so far taken to save Halvergate Marshes, for instance, have a lot to do with members of Friends of the Earth sitting down in front of tractors and rather little to do with the natural inclinations of government. Only if as much pressure as possible is exerted on behalf of conservation, not just by specialist groups but by the public at large, will any significant part of the countryside be saved. A small but heartening news story in August 1985 told of householders and their children in Cheshire standing in front of a bulldozer to save the meadow near their homes from being covered with waste from the building of a bypass.

What we should all be demanding from the government is a decisive move away from the balancing of interests, from voluntary guidelines and gentlemen's agreements, towards firm legislation that would make damaging the environment extremely unprofitable. It is not for me to say what form this should take, but there is no shortage of concerned and authoritative advice available if the government can be persuaded to listen to it. I am sure, though, that it is only through legislaton and a massive diversion of funds away from feather-bedding farmers into a national strategy for saving the countryside that the tide of destruction can begin to be stemmed.

If the tone of this book sometimes seems strident, this is only a reflection of the urgency I feel about saving the places and wildlife that I paint. I cannot bear the thought that some day I might have to paint them from memory.

Gordon Beningfield
Water End
Hertfordshire

September 1985

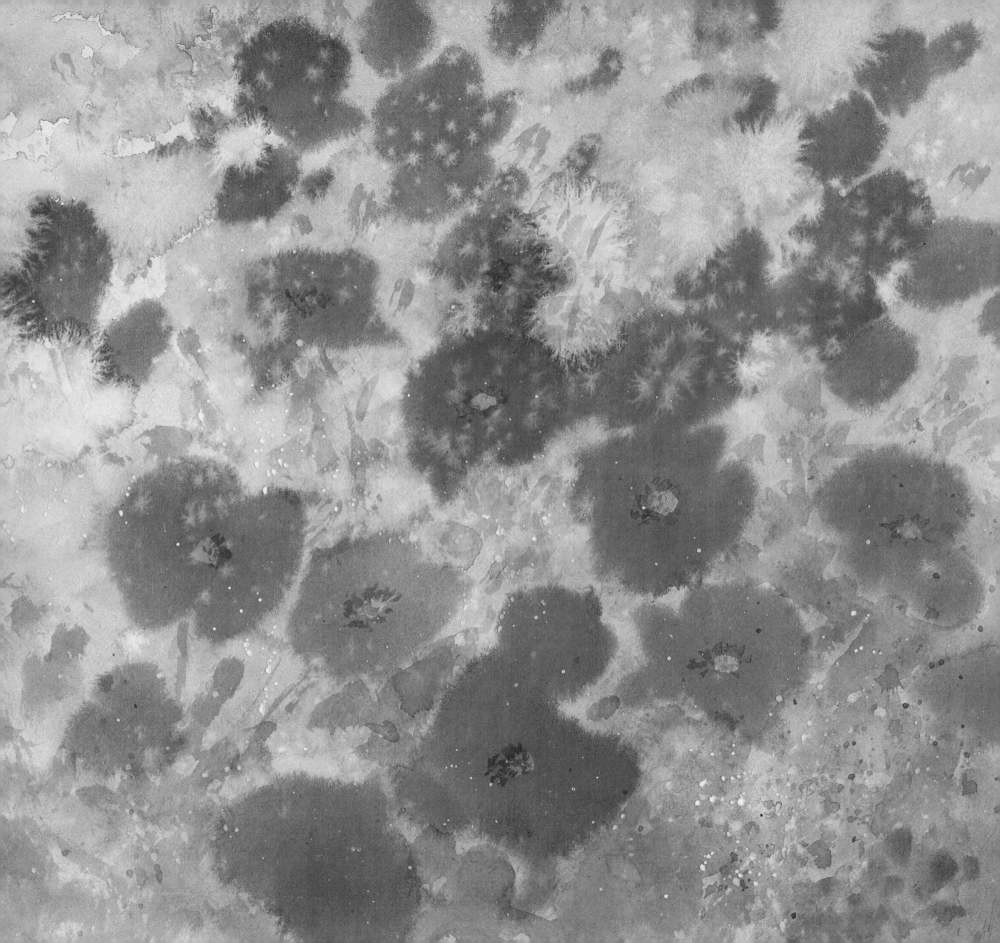